A New True Book

PEACOCKS AND PEAHENS

By Joan Kalbacken

CHILDRENS PRESS®
CHICAGO

A peahen and her chick

PHOTO CREDITS

© Reinhard Brucker–21, Field Museum, Chicago, 9 (left); Milwaukee Public Museum, 9 (right)

Photri–© James Kirby, 6 (bottom right); © B. Kulik, 27

H. Armstrong Roberts–© George Hunter, 33

Root Resources–© Kenneth W. Fink, 6 (bottom left)

© James P. Rowan, 29

Tom Stack & Associates–© Thomas Kitchin, 15, 44

Tony Stone Images–© John Warden, Cover, 36; © Tony Craddock, 4; © Leonard Lee Rue III, 7, 16; © Norbert Wu, 11; © L.T. Rhodes, 34

SuperStock International, Inc.–© Ron Dahlquist, 41 (left)

Valan–© J.A. Wilkinson, 2, 41 (right); © Stephen John Krasemann, 6 (top left); © Bob Gurr, 6 (top right), 25; © Kennon Cooke, 20, 31; © Michael J. Johnson, 30; © Jane K. Hugesson, 32; © Aubrey Lang, 35 (left); © John Cancalosi, 35 (right); © J.R. Page, 38; © Dr. A. Farquhar, 45

VIREO–© Sid Lipschutz, 14

Visuals Unlimited–© D. Long, 13; © John D. Cunningham, 19; © M. Long, 22; © Ron Somer, 24; © D. Cavagnaro, 43

COVER: Peacock showing feathers (mating display behavior)

Project Editor: Fran Dyra
Design: Margrit Fiddle

Library of Congress Cataloging-in-Publication Data

Kalbacken, Joan.
  Peacocks and peahens / by Joan Kalbacken.
    p.   cm.–(A New true book)
  Includes index.
  ISBN 0-516-01070-0
  1. Peafowl–Juvenile literature.   [1.   Peacocks.]
I. Title.
QL696.G27K34   1994
598.6'.17–dc20
                              94-10946
                                CIP
                                AC

TABLE OF CONTENTS

PEACOCKS AND PEAHENS

Have you ever seen a big bird with "eyes" on its feathers? These beautiful birds are male peafowl, called peacocks. Female peafowl are called peahens—and they don't have those fancy feathers. But many people call all these birds "peacocks."

Peafowl belong to the Phasianidae family.

Pheasants, turkeys, chickens, and guinea fowl (clockwise from top left) are peafowl relatives.

Pheasants, turkeys, guinea fowl, and chickens are other members of this family.

The male peafowl is famous for its beautiful train—a huge fan of

The stiff, sharp spur above a peafowl's foot is used for protection.

brightly colored feathers
that it can spread out over
its back. Only male
peafowl have a train.

Peafowl have white,
featherless legs. Each leg
has a spur–a stiff, sharp

spine—above the foot.
Each foot has four toes
with strong claws.

Peafowl are native to
India, Southeast Asia, and
parts of the East Indies.
Their large size and rich
colors have been admired
by the people of these
lands for thousands of
years.

A Japanese *inro* (left) with a peacock design. An *inro* is a small container worn on a sash around the waist that was used to carry medicine or perfume. Right: A Chinese vase decorated with a peacock.

PEAFOWL TRAVEL THE WORLD

In ancient times, peafowl were carried to many parts of the world. They were given as gifts to nobles and kings.

Historians think that Phoenician traders carried peafowl to Egypt as early as 1000 B.C. The Egyptian pharaohs kept the beautiful birds to decorate their gardens.

The ancient Romans thought the birds were magical. Because peafowl were so pretty, Romans thought they also might be good to eat, and it was true! Wealthy Romans served the costly birds at special banquets.

An Indian peacock at a zoo in Atlanta, Georgia. The Indian peafowl is sometimes called the "common" or "blue" peafowl.

In some countries, people still hunt and trap peafowl for food. But more often they are sold for their beauty. Today, peafowl are admired in zoos, parks, and gardens all over the world.

PEAFOWL SPECIES

Ornithologists—scientists who study birds—have learned much about peafowl. Two species live in Asia—the Indian peafowl and the Javan peafowl.

The Indian peafowl is the best-known species. It is the national bird of India. The government there protects the birds, and they run free in villages and towns. These birds prefer grassy, open land with few trees.

Javan peafowl live in Thailand and Southeast Asia as far south as the island of Java. They have a longer neck and legs

The Javan peafowl is also known as the "green" peafowl.

Congo peafowl live in Africa. They were discovered by scientists in the early 1900s.

and a slimmer body than Indian peafowl.

The Congo peafowl is found in the forests of Africa. Some ornithologists think the Congo peafowl is really a kind of pheasant. But it is closely related to the Asian peafowl.

PLUME COLORS AND TRAINS

Peafowl are noted for their bright feathers, or plumes. The Indian peacock has a bluish green head with white patches near his eyes. He has a small brush of

The Indian peacock's "crown" is a brush of blue feathers.

15

It is easy to tell peacocks and peahens apart
because of the peacock's long train.

blue feathers as a crown.
His wings are brown with
touches of black. His body
is gray or brown.

The Indian peahen has

16

a brownish head and a

white neck. Her breast
and back are brown with
specks of green.

Javan peafowl are
mostly green with some
bronze-colored feathers.
They have a crest of long
green plumes.

The Javan peacock and
peahen are similar in color.
But the female can be
recognized easily. She is
the one without the train.

Congo peafowl are quite
different from Asian
peafowl in size and color.

They are much smaller. Their tails are short. And they have no feathers on their necks. Congo peacocks have shiny black plumes, but no train. The peahens are reddish brown and green.

Peacocks can spread their train straight up into a beautiful fan-shaped display. A peacock's train is made up of over 200

When a peacock walks along the ground, its long train trails behind.

plumes that grow from the lower back. Some trains trail 5 to 6 feet (1.5 to 1.8 meters) behind the bird.

Many people think that the train is the peacock's tail. But the real tail is made up of short feathers beneath the train.

Small feathers called coverts grow between the train and the tail. When the coverts are raised, they lift the long plumes of the fan.

This view shows the peacock's train, the smaller dark-colored coverts, and the white tail feathers.

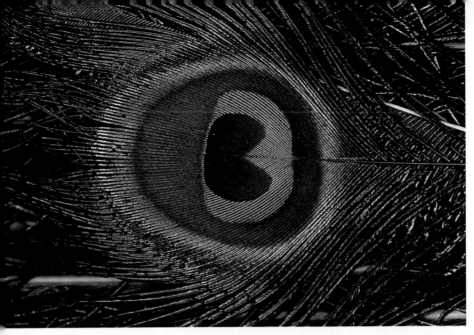

Close-up of
an eyespot

DO FEATHERS HAVE EYES?

When a peacock spreads his fan, hundreds of "eyes" seem to appear on the feathers. These eyespots, called "ocelli," are deep-blue circles surrounded by greenish blue and golden brown rings.

21

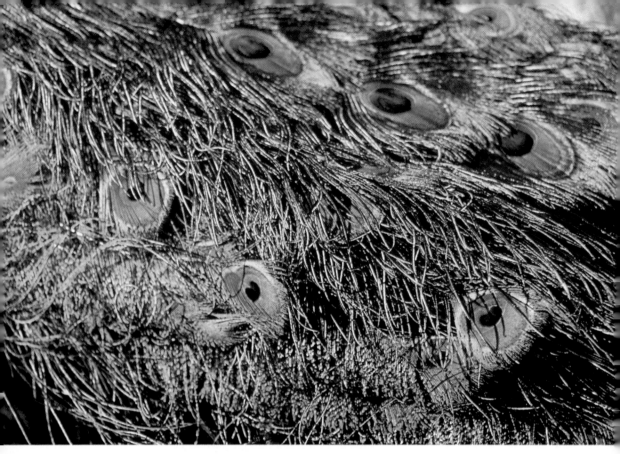

A peacock's train, showing the many shifting colors

The ocelli seem to glow. Their many tiny feathers have iridescent, rainbow-like colors. The colors reflect sunlight, and they change as the peacock moves.

MATING HABITS

Indian and Javan peacocks are polygamous. This means they mate with more than one peahen. Sometimes males have as many as five or six hens. Congo peacocks are monogamous. They have only one mate.

In fall, peacocks begin to grow their beautiful long train feathers. By spring, they are ready to mate. To get the attention of the

A male peacock calls to get the attention of the hens.

hens, the males call day and night. Their call is a loud, harsh screech.

Soon the peacocks begin to spread their trains in a wide fan. They strut in front of the peahens. They spend hours rattling their trains to

The peacock tries to attract the peahens by showing his beautiful fan.

attract the hens. The females often pretend not to notice.

In late summer, the peahens mate with the peacocks. After mating, the peacocks begin to molt, or shed their feathers.

25

THE CHICKS ARRIVE

Peahens lay their eggs in a nest hidden in a hollow tree stump, tall grass, or shrubbery. The eggs are tan or greenish white and sometimes speckled. After she lays three to six eggs, the peahen spreads her feathers over them. Then she settles down over the eggs to keep them warm.

It takes twenty-eight days for the eggs to

hatch. Baby peafowl, called chicks, are covered with fuzzy, light feathers. Their wings are darker.

A peahen with a tiny chick

27

Peahens are good mothers. They cover the chicks with their feathers to keep them warm and dry.

Within one week, the chicks are able to fly a little. Within a month, small crests appear on the tops of their heads. Soon their long, colorful plumes begin to grow.

This chick is growing fast. Soon it will be on its own.

The mothers feed the babies from their mouths until the chicks can peck their own food from the ground. Chicks eat seeds, grubs, and insects.

Peafowl use their strong claws to dig for food.

EATING

Peafowl eat leaves, fruit, flowers, and small animals like frogs, mice, and snakes.

Peafowl have no teeth, so they cannot chew their food. When they swallow, the food goes into a pouch called a crop. There it is ground up before passing on to the stomach.

The peacock's long train makes flying difficult. The birds usually stay on the ground.

ROOSTING AND PREENING

Peafowl move slowly.
They prefer to stay in the
same feeding grounds and
watering places. They feed
on the ground in the
morning and afternoon.

31

Peafowl roost in the lower branches of trees.

When the sun begins to set, they fly to a low branch and roost there for the night.

Indian and Javan peacocks do not fly well. Their long trains are heavy. It is hard for them to fly quickly or very high. Flying is easier for the Congo peafowl, which has no train.

Some peafowl are white. This one lives at Ardastra Gardens at Nassau in the Bahamas.

Because their legs are long, the peacocks can hardly keep their balance in a strong wind. When they spread their trains in the wind, they sway and strut to keep from falling down.

A white peafowl preening its feathers

Peafowl spend a lot of time preening, or cleaning themselves. Their long neck allows them to reach all parts of their body. They use their beak to fluff and smooth their feathers. Then they rub oil over their feathers. The oil comes from an oil gland in front of their tail.

PREDATORS AND OTHER DANGERS

Their large size and bright colors make wild peafowl easy prey for leopards, tigers, and other large animals. Their eggs are a tasty meal for raccoons and foxes.

Leopards (left) and tigers are some of the predators that hunt peacocks.

But peafowl have keen hearing and excellent eyesight. When an enemy comes near, they quickly fly away to a safe place. Sometimes they fight off predators with their sharp claws and spurs.

Indian peafowl are hardy birds. They can live in places where the temperature falls below zero. But the chicks cannot live through sudden changes in temperature.

Javan peafowl are not as strong as Indian peafowl. They must live in a warm climate. They are not protected by laws like the Indian birds, and their survival is threatened as people move into the areas where they live.

Peafowl live in parks and gardens all over the world.
This one struts its stuff in Vancouver, Canada.

PEOPLE AND PEAFOWL

Most people enjoy watching peacocks spread their trains in a huge fan. Most of us delight in the bright colors and eyespots of these beautiful birds. But even a peacock can't please everyone.

Some people are angry with the big birds, especially in a town called Rolling Hills near Los Angeles, California. Seventy years ago, the town had only six peafowl. Today, more than one hundred fifty of the beautiful birds live in Rolling Hills.

But the peafowl keep people up at night. The birds screech and call to their mates. They take

Peacocks in towns and cities can cause trouble by eating flowers and other garden plants (right). Their screeching (left) keeps people awake at night.

food set out for pets. They eat flowers and garden plants. Peafowl droppings cover the sidewalks, roofs, and yards. Residents have to clean up the mess.

Even so, some of the people in Rolling Hills are happy to have these special birds. Tourists come from faraway places to see the peafowl. And tourists help business. They buy gifts in the stores and eat in the restaurants.

An Indian peacock spreads his fan for a hen.
Does she look interested?

THE FUTURE OF PEAFOWL

When you visit a zoo,
look for the peafowl. When
the peacock sees you, he
may even strut before you,
showing off his beautiful

43

Peafowl are safe from predators in zoos, parks, and gardens.

train. Then you'll know why we say "proud as a peacock."

There is little danger of these proud birds ever becoming extinct. In the

safety of zoos, parks, and
places like Rolling Hills,
the beautiful peafowl will
continue to strut and show
off their fancy feathers.

WORDS YOU SHOULD KNOW

coverts (KOH • verts)–small feathers between a peacock's train and its tail

crop (KRAHP)–a pouch in front of a bird's stomach where food is ground up

display (dis • PLAY)–to show off something

extinct (ex • TINKT)–no longer living

gland (GLAND)–a special body part that makes things that the body can use or give off

grubs (GRUHBZ)–larvae; an early form of an insect that looks like a short, fat worm

guinea fowl (GHIN • ee FOWL)–a bird like a chicken; it has dark feathers with white spots

hardy (HAR • dee)–able to live in climates that have harsh winters

historian (hiss • TOR • ee • yun)–a person who studies what people have said and done in the past

iridescent (eer • ih • DES • int)–having many changing colors

molt (MOHLT)–to shed feathers or fur

monogamous (muh • NAH • guh • muss)–having only one mate

ocelli (oh • SEH • ly)–colored spots that look like eyes

ornithologist (or • nih • THAHL • uh • jist)–a scientist who studies birds

pharaoh (FAIR • oh)–a ruler in ancient Egypt

Phasianidae (faz • ee • ON • ih • day)–the family that includes peafowl, turkeys, chickens, etc.

pheasant (FEZ • int)–a brightly colored bird with long tail feathers

Phoenician (fih • NEE • shin)–one of a trading people that lived on the eastern Mediterranean shore thousands of years ago

plumes (PLOOMZ)–feathers

polygamous (puh • LIG • uh • muss)–having more than one mate

predator (PREH • dih • ter)–an animal that kills and eats other animals

preening (PREE • ning)–cleaning and oiling the feathers

reflect (rih • FLEKT)–to throw back light from a surface

species (SPEE • seez)–a group of related plants or animals that are able to interbreed

spur (SPER)–a sharp spine on a bird's leg

tourists (TOOR • ists)–people who travel and enjoy seeing new places and meeting different people.

INDEX

About the Author

Joan Formell Kalbacken earned a BA in education from the University of Wisconsin, Madison. After graduate work at Coe College, Iowa, and the University of Toulouse, France, she received an MA from Illinois State University, Normal, Illinois. She was a secondary school teacher in Beloit, Wisconsin, and Pekin and Normal, Illinois. She taught French and mathematics for twenty-nine years and she also served as foreign language supervisor in Normal. She received the award for excellence in Illinois' program, "Those Who Excel."

She is past state president of the Delta Kappa Gamma Society International and a member of Pi Delta Phi, Kappa Delta Pi, AAUW, and Phi Delta Kappa.